M000197675

''He who runs in every man perishes his life, just as the soul that runs in all souls perishes its spirit.'' — Biték

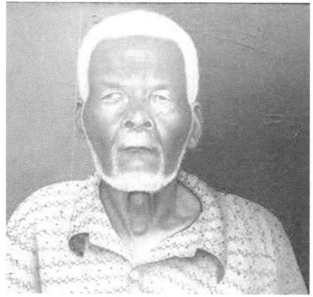

Photo of Biték

Publisher's Review

'What would you do if you couldn't die no matter how much danger you're in? If you couldn't stop until your life's mission is accomplished? How would you negotiate divine mandates and human adventures? **Biték** is a condensed cross-cultural tale of a man with a divine assignment: to save his village from the hands of colonisation. This is an expository account of European colonisation's religious beliefs, laws, blatant violations and historical aggressions geared towards eradicating the cultural identity of Biték's African ancestors. Moreover, this book demonstrates the developed political, social, spiritual and religious system Biték's African ancestors had before violations of their natural rights in all kinds. As an exhumation of a great African tradition buried by European colonisation, **Biték** presents a vibrant appeal for the protection and preservation of world heritage.'

Pierced Rock Press

PRAISE FOR *BITÉK*

'*A story of a simple man with an extraordinary will to live and let live.*'
– Jericka P. Orellano, Managing Editor, Lexcode Philippines

'*An extraordinary contribution to the exhumation and understanding of our tradition buried by colonization.*'
– Mbombog Mbeleg, patriarch and traditional priest of the Basaa tradition

'*This is a book of wisdom.*'
– Mbombog Mbenda, patriarch and custodian of the Basaa tradition

'*This is a unique and fascinating book — wonderful storytelling that grips your attention, together with a razor-sharp deconstruction of the damage inflicted by European colonization on the life, culture and spiritual traditions of the author's African ancestors … I wholeheartedly recommend this book to you — independent of your cultural background and spiritual understanding.*"
– Rev. Dr. David Keizan Scott Roshi, Founder, StoneWater Zen Sangha, United Kingdom

Rev. Dr. David Keizan Scott Roshi is the founder and leader of StoneWater Zen Sangha. He is an ordained Buddhist priest and lineage holder at Sōtō Zen school, having received Shiho (Dharma transmission) from Tenshin Fletcher Roshi in October 2009. Keizan is also a widely published writer, with works about Japan, Zen Buddhism, comparative religion and cookery.

BITÉK

He From Whom Death Ran

Massocki Ma Massocki

Pierced Rock Press

Pierced Rock Press

www.piercedrockpress.com

Copyright ©2020 Massocki Ma Massocki

All rights reserved.

No part of this publication may be reproduced, stored in a retrieval system or transmitted in any form or by any means — electronically, mechanically, photocopying, recording or otherwise — without the prior written permission of the publisher.

Paperback ISBN: 978-9956-465-07-1
eBook ISBN: 978-9956-465-08-8
Hardcover ISBN: 978-9956-465-09-5

Cover by: Bienvenido Junior Swinton
Interior by : Rohit Graphic Desinger

Pierced Rock Press is the publishing outfit of Pierced Rock, a conglomeration of companies involved in art and mass media production.

Our mission is to promote human rights in general — African people's rights, in particular — and advance African literature.

Thank you for buying an authorised copy of this book. You are sustaining our important work and ensuring that the press achieves its mission.

Pierced Rock Press is committed to publishing works of quality and integrity. In this spirit, we are proud to offer this book to our readers; however, the story, experiences and words are those of the author alone.

About the Author

Massocki Ma Massocki is a columnist and activist aligned to pan-Africanism. He writes for digital and print news media and regional and international organisations.

Massocki also promotes pan-Africanism conversations and conferences in Europe, Asia and Africa, deliberately recounting Africa's history by retelling its stories through people's witness accounts. His first book, *The Pride of an African Migrant*, was published in 2020 by Pierced Rock Press.

www.massockimamassocki.com

DEDICATION

BITÉK is dedicated to the man whose story it tells: Biték bi Bimai. Rest in peace and power, Grandpa.

This book is also for my deceased great-grandfather Mbombog Ndjami, without whom I would have never existed to write this book.

Before I was born, my mother gave birth to two stillborn babies. As such, when my mother conceived me, she was sure I would not survive. However, one night, while my mother was three months pregnant, Mbombog Ndjami, who had died several years before my birth, appeared to my mother and said,

'The child you carry must be born, and that is why I came. In the backyard, you'll find a snail shell. Retrieve this at sunrise, and leave it under your bed during your pregnancy. Then, go to the village Ndog Mbog, and tell the patriarchs that I have asked you be bathed on my grave at two o'clock in the morning. This is so this child will be born.'

The next day, my mother followed everything my deceased great-grandfather instructed. This is how my mother gave birth to me prematurely at seven months. After my birth, he appeared before my mother once again and gave her a stone, which he also ordered to be put under her bed.

Acknowledgement

My deepest gratitude goes to my father, Massocki Ma Biték, who shared his father's adventures with me. Without him, Biték would not have been written.

Photo of my father, Massocki Ma Biték

AUTHOR'S NOTE

The events described in this book are based on the life of my grandfather, Biték Bi Bimai, as narrated by my father. Texts of some conversations were also extracted from secondary sources to provide their closest possible interpretation. The picture on the front cover shows a 90-year-old Biték, drawn by Basecal, a Cameroonian artist.

While escaping from Nigeria in 1933, my grandfather left his two sons and never saw them again. Through this book, my family and I hope to connect with our relatives in Nigeria who we have yet to meet.

TABLE OF CONTENTS

CHAPTER 1
BITÉK IS BORN

In the 15th century, Portuguese explorers reached the coast of the Mbende River and found flocks of shrimps, leading them to name the area Rio dos Camarões, meaning the river of shrimps. Later, it became Cameroon, a country in West Africa located in the southern coastal area, where the village of Ndog Mbog stands.

Ndog Mbog is inhabited by the Ngok Lituba tribe of the Basaa people, and their major occupations included fishing, farming and hunting. They lived in homes made of mud and were described as mostly peaceful, having developed a political, social, spiritual and religious system known as Mbog.

The Ngok Lituba people emigrated from Egypt, fleeing in 525 BC when the Assyrians and King Cambyses II of Persia raided their ancestral land. They found refuge in a cave at a rocky mountain called Ngok Lituba in Cameroon and dispersed across the new land to build new homes.

It is believed that the ancient Egyptian civilization is only a reproduction of one that had always existed in the metaphysical sphere: Ngok Lituba, a meteorite with a one-kilometre diameter that fell from space at least two million years ago.

After having fled Egypt because of the invasion, they began looking for the meteorite. It was only in the 9th century that they found Ngok Lituba and sought refuge within it after being pursued by enemies.

According to the Basaa mythology, the Basaa people were still being pursued upon arriving at Ngok Lituba. To lose their enemies, they hid inside a cave (Ngok Lituba). The entrance to the cave had gotten covered by a large spiderweb. Because of this, the people chasing them did not pay heed to the cave, thinking that the web could not have been there if people had entered it. This is why the spider called 'Libôbôl' is intrinsically symbolic among the Basaa of Ngok Lituba and why their ancestors forbade killing spiders.

'Ngok' means 'rock', and 'Lituba' means 'hole'. Thus, the term 'Ngok Lituba' literally means a rock with a hole or a pierced rock. In some translations, however, it could also refer to a woman's vulva.

Ngok Lituba symbolises the goddess Isis, the most ancient god in Egyptian mythology. Hence, she is most revered by the Ngok Lituba people, who call her 'Hilolombi', meaning the most ancient of ancients. Ancient Egyptian scripture confirms that Isis was discovered in a rock, which is why Ngok Lituba was designated as a holy sanctuary and pilgrimage site. An ancient city in Egypt was also named Saa, another name for Isis. This is why the Ngok Lituba people call themselves Basaa, meaning those of Saa or Isis.

The word 'mountain' is mentioned 500 times in the Bible, 'stone', 370 times and 'rock', 142 times. Below are a few passages in the Bible referring to stone, rock and mountain.

> — The LORD is my rock, fortress and deliverer; my God is my rock, in

whom I take refuge, my shield and the horn of my salvation, my stronghold.

— And I tell you that you are Peter, and on this rock I will build my church, and the gates of Hades will not overcome it.

— Therefore, thus says the Lord God, 'Behold, I am the one who has laid as a foundation in Zion, a stone, a tested stone, a precious cornerstone, of a sure foundation: "Whoever believes will not be in haste."'

— Why do you gaze in envy, O mountains of many peaks? This is the mountain God chose for His dwelling, where the LORD will surely dwell forever.

These may explain why the holy sanctuary is the subject of dispute between Cameroon's Roman Catholic Church and the Basaa people, the legitimate and historical owners of the site captured in 1958 during European colonisation. To this day, the site is yet to be returned to the Basaa people despite numerous letters addressed to the Vatican.

Before the proliferation of colonisation and its religion, the Basaa people practiced a traditional religion known as Mbog under the leadership of a patriarch and a priest called Mbombog.

These patriarchs fall under the lineage of Egyptian kings known as pharaohs, alluding to one reason they are called Mbombog. The term 'Mbombog' is a contraction of the words 'Mbom' and 'Mbog'. 'Mbom' means python or forehead (The kings of ancient Egypt, wore the snake symbol on their foreheads.), while 'Mbog' refers to the universe, tradition, history, geographical area and so on.

A Mbombog is a patriarch and a traditional priest who inherited the tradition from ancestors and can consult them. In the Basaa culture, the universe is called Mbog, and according to the people of Ngok Lituba, Mbog has no beginning and end. Without a beginning and an end, Mbog has created itself. It is the energy behind everything, and all things exist within Mbog.

Death is merely an illusion that veils the reality of life. It serves as a way to continually remind humans of life's vanity, prompting them to live moral and conscious lives. A frequently quoted Ngok Lituba proverb philosophises thus.

'Dead people are not dead; we fear death because we are attached to our human desires and scared of the unknown.'

The veil between the 'dead' and the 'living' is thin; the former realm influences the latter. However, the privilege to do so is only reserved for those who, upon death, are elevated to ancestorship.

Ancestors have the power to intercede for humans. However, not everyone becomes an ancestor. They are those who, after death, unite with Ta-Ra. Ra is the divinity of the sun in ancient Egypt, who is also referred to as Father Ra or Ta-Ra.

The Basaa people venerate the divinity of the sun because without the sun there would be no life on earth. The Sun warms our seas, generates our weather patterns, and gives energy to the growing green plants that provide the food and oxygen for life on Earth.

The dead must unite with Ta-Ra to be conferred with ancestorship. This is why the Ngok Lituba people call ancestors Tara. Only those who have led good lives until a ripe old age, died a good death and were accorded full burial rites can become ancestors or Tara.

Ancestors were often regarded as Mbombog on Earth. Now that they have been veiled from the living, they remain as Mbombog only within the land of the spirits. They continue their role as liaisons in death and do not cease from concerning themselves with their families' general welfare. However, as they are no longer visible physically, some enhanced powerful elements are attributed to them. Transcending physical limitations, ancestors gain more potential and significantly enhance their dignity, power and prestige in death. They also possess considerable powers for good. Thus, it is essential to remain on good terms with them and offer more than they were due when they were still alive on Earth. Ancestors are the guardians of traditional morality, thereby commanding high respect for traditional laws and customs.

In 1882, in the Ndog Mbog village's forest, referred to as 'Mbandi', the second of the three wives of a man named Bimai bi Maa gave birth to a boy. According to Ngok Lituba tradition, the act of naming newborns falls under the responsibility of ancestors, not that of the children's parents.

Following this, Bimai bi Maa ran to Som, a patriarch known as a Mbombog (the python of the universe), to announce that his second wife had delivered a baby boy and know the name of his new son. To keep up with customs and traditions, stating that people should not meet with a Mbombog empty-handed, Bimai bi Maa brought the best palm wine and kola nuts he could find — two symbolic items of great importance that, when given together, signified meaningful negotiations, conversations and celebrations.

Mbombog Som opened his Gambi, which means 'oracle', his channel between the visible and the invisible world, to consult ancestors on behalf of Bimai bi Maa. The oracle advised that Bimai Bi Maa's son shall be named Biték, which means 'soil', because Biték will save his village. Mbombog Som then relayed the ancestors' message to Bimai Bi Maa. According to tradition, Mbombog Som asked Bimai Bi Maa to go home that day and wait for him until the next morning at his house before sunrise.

At home, Mbombog Som always had all sorts of people working for him. According to tradition, on that same day, he ordered his woodworker to make a wooden pot immediately and have it ready before the next sunrise. So, it was said, and so, it was done. The following day, Mbombog Som had another order: to bring before him a young female virgin before sunrise.

Again, it was done. Mbombog Som gave the newly constructed wooden pot to the girl and ordered her to fetch water from the nearest river or stream and return before sunrise. This was also done.

News of Bimai Bi Maa's newborn had spread throughout the village. Before sunrise, the whole Mbandi community of the Ndog Mbog village gathered at Bimai Bi Maa's house to celebrate with the family and partake in the traditional naming ceremony.

At the celebration, Mbombog Som stood while carrying a kola nut; a traditional broom known as Jai li Mbog, which represents the visible world and power and is carried only by a Mbombog; a staff symbolizing the invisible world and a traditional bag known as Mbot i Mbog, transferred from one patriarch to another and contained traditional relics called Bi bang bi Mbog.

The young female virgin brought before Mbombog Som the wooden pot brimming with water, bowed and gave it to him before being blessed and dismissed. Afterwards, Mbombog Som put the Bi bang bi Mbog mixed with herbs and plants called Mabui into the wooden pot.

Mbombog Som proceeded to honour the ancestry of Mbombogs before him in a poetic recital of his claim to legitimacy as the rightful heir of the traditional heritage.

He then called on the names of the nine Mbombogs before him, saying,

'Mbongo transmitted Mbog to Ngom.

Ngom transmitted Mbog to Mbog.

Mbog transmitted Mbog to Ndjéé.

Ndjéé transmitted Mbog to Nguimbus.

Nguimbus transmitted Mbog to Banyemel.

Banyemel transmitted Mbog to Mbagaa.

Mbagaa transmitted Mbog to Ikemb.

Ikemb transmitted Mbog to Makani.

Makani transmitted Mbog to me.'

The crowd nodded in acknowledgement of each ancestral priest, with some even bowing in deference and humming in agreement. Ancestors duly referenced, Mbombog Som called for the newborn. In front of the assembly, Bimai bi Maa and his second wife carried their baby, bowed and handed the child to Mbombog Som to begin with the birth rites to be bestowed upon their boy, following Ngok Lituba tradition.

To start, Mbombog Som eulogised the universe.

'Mbog eeh!'

'Mbog eeh!'

'Mbog eeh!'

The assembly responded with *'Sai'* to each salutation.

Mbombog Som then introduced the newborn to the nine Ngok Lituba ancestors. They are the nine patriarchs that led the Ngok Lituba people after taking refuge in the cave.

Ngok

Mbog

Njel

Mbang

Mban

Ngaa

Nsaa

Bias

Buwe

The ancestor said,

'Blessing with water and the kola nut that we call "Sai i Mbog" is the heritage of Hilolombi, the most ancient of ancients.'

Holding the baby in his hands, Mbombog Som poured water from the wooden pot onto the child's head. Afterwards, he began to prophesise about the life of Bimai bi Maa's son.

'Hilolombi, the most ancient of ancients, the supreme divinity, will bless you with many children. You will see your grandchildren. You will live long, and so many times will death run away from you. You are the man from whom death ran away. You will save the people of the Ndog Mbog village from the hands of its enemies.'

After Mbombog Som touched the baby's head with his Jai li Mbog three times, he said,

'You shall accomplish your destiny.'

With a kola nut in his hands, he continued,

'The kola nut symbolises the love between humans and divinities and that among human beings.'

Mbombog Som bit a piece of the kola nut, chewed it into paste and smeared it on the baby's face. He then lifted the child into the air and presented him to the sun, proclaiming,

'You shall be called "Biték". You shall be called "Biték". You shall be called "Biték".'

And the whole assembly responded,

'Biték is his name.'

Addressing the gathered crowd, Mbombog Som said, *'Me pot me mal. Baa pena a ye?'* (So be it. Is there any objection?)

The assembly responded in a chorus. *'Pena a ta ye.'* (No objections.)

Afterwards, Mbombog Som returned the baby to his parents and ordered for palm wine and rice, which he immediately received. He then poured a small amount on the ground as a symbol of gratitude to ancestors.

'The traditional dance may now begin.'

With this, Mbombog Som officially closed the naming rites and started the fete to celebrate Biték's birth. The women performed Koo, a traditional dance, and other guests approached Biték's mother to welcome the newborn.

Biték was the fifth child in the family. He had six brothers and one sister whose beauty earned her the title of queen. Many hectares of land were also given to her in exchange for her hand in marriage. Biték himself was handsome too, with some even saying that he was one of the village's best-looking men.

Like all young men in Ndog Mbog, Biték learnt farming, fishing and hunting as he grew. He took a liking to hunting, eventually becoming highly skilled in the craft. Most nights, Biték and other youth would gather around flaming firewood to hear words of wisdom from Mbombog Som. The latter would often tell fables, and one particularly intrigued Biték. It was the story of a hunter named Sudman, which went like this.

Once upon a time, there was a great hunter named Sudman who always killed antelopes. Each time he killed one, he would hang its antlers on his bedroom wall to admire them before he goes to bed and when he wakes up.

One day, Sudman became curious about his death, so he consulted a Mbombog to know how he would die. The Mbombog opened his Gambi, consulted ancestors on behalf of Sudman and revealed that antelopes would take their revenge and kill him.

To avoid his fate, Sudman decided to stop hunting and going near bushes, saying, 'Let's see how an antelope can kill me now.' However, one night, while he was sleeping, one of the antlers hanging on the ceiling fell, hitting Sudman on the chest and eventually killing him.

Oh, young men. Listen to your ancestors. They know the past, present and future.

Whoever forgets his ancestors will also be overlooked by his progeny.

Oh, young men. You may walk faster than the old, but you do not know the way.

A seated elder sees farther than a standing young man.

Oh, young men. The words of ancestors shall always come to pass.

CHAPTER 2
THE MBANDI ATTACK

On the 12th of July 1884, Germany and Baluba's chiefs signed the German–Douala treaty. According to Germany, the treaty legalised the colonisation of the area known today as Cameroon. Germany claimed that the Baluba chiefs represented the entire Cameroon population that was, in fact, an aggregate of many self-governing and self-determining tribes. The authority of a tribe's monarchy and chiefdom was valid only within the cultural and religious traditions that established it and for the people within its territorial boundaries.

Reflecting on these events, Michel Kounou notes in his book, *Le Panafricanisme: De La Crise à la Renaissance,*

> *Native chiefs who have affixed their crosses under a German text were neither sovereign nor empowered to sign. Bored by gifts, drunk or constrained, they were barely aware of what they had done ... Often, agents of companies, explorers or adventurers also drafted agreements for the needs of their cause and deliberately cheated blacks. When ratifying or rejecting draft treaties, governments were essentially inspired by their use to defeat other European claims. It was necessary to legitimise this political brutality and give oneself a good conscience by extorting treaties from African leaders. Treaties are seen as essential cogs in the colonial occupation.*

Germany's colonisation birthed an era of forced labour, oppression and varying forms of inhumanity. There was one primary rule: the colonial power could go as deep as it wanted into the land until another colonial power presented itself. It owned the land and its peoples and could do with them whatever it pleased.

In 1896, German forces fought a bloody war against the Babimbi Empire. Villages were captured, houses razed and residents slaughtered. The deadliest battles were fought in the Mbandi forest when the carnage reached Ndog Mbog. Biték was only 14 years old then and, along with his family, included in those displaced from their homes in the forest.

Biték's family became refugees in the village centre. This experience of running for survival, Biték would later realise, was simply the first of many. It was initiation—a glimpse of adventures fate had lined up for his future.

Escaping the Mbandi forest, Biték's family left behind livestock, fruits and vegetables. They were in the company of many other families who had also chosen to run and survive without looking back rather than pack their belongings.

At the village centre, they faced famine. The land was dry and uncultivated, and the only food available was kola nut. They consoled each other with chants of tomél, meaning 'at least, kola nuts'. As such, their new land was named Tomél, and they became the Tomél people.

Biték woke every morning to gather kola nuts for the family's meal. After breakfast, he and his family would work the clay to build the family home, which was completed after several months.

CHAPTER 3
A SHRED OF BOYHOOD

Ndog Mbog was frightening when night fell. Leopards roared, and gorillas grunted.

The Song Lolo waterfalls rushed, splashed and cadenced into running murmurs. Unknown wild animals punctuated the dark with their songs and calls, tones and timbres.

The young mind went wild, imagining mischievous ghosts from evening tales, exploring the night, tiptoeing into huts and waiting around corners to smack the buttocks of wandering youngsters.

Despite these, the youth sat around, burning firewood every night and begging for mythical stories from willing elders before the moon sat in the skies and parents fetched them, signalling bedtime. The nights were even scarier when Biték had to journey across rivers or slink around in forests.

The village was located in a big forest. Roads were mere paths where the grass had been cut. The village centre was less like a forest, strewn as it was with huts and other human structures. Away from settlements, the forest pulsed with danger. Wild animals prowled unrestrained. Traps littered the floor, lying in wait for unsuspecting meat.

Majestic trees, colourful flowers and melodious birds enchanted young minds, seduced untrained feet and swallowed paths that led back home. Mastery of forest walkways was, therefore, imperative. It stacked the bets higher for the safe return of one who had gone fishing or hunting at night.

Bimai Bi Maa taught Biték to prowl the forest. Over many nights and expeditions, he showed his son animal traps and how to avoid them. He also primed him to distinguish trees' characteristics, recognise them at night and find his way with their guidance. He also taught the young one to face wild animals and survive, signs that he was lost in the forest and what he must do.

Fishing and hunting were deemed best at dusk and essential for survival in Ndog Mbog. They defined manhood as much as circumcision, wrestling prowess and back-burning with a melting machete. With other activities, they were mastered before adulthood.

Melting machete was considered barbaric by the same Germans who waged bloody wars to capture Cameroon. They eventually declared it forbidden to make the colonised people least resistant to foreign rule, so they could quell practices that could rouse strength and bravery among the natives.

One morning, Biték's father woke unusually early. He sharpened a knife, threw it into a fire he had stoked and requested Biték's mother to keep the fire burning while he went to the bush.

Biték's mother fed the flame with small wood chunks and charcoal to keep it alight. The fire was still burning, and the sharpened knife remained in the fire when Biték's father returned with medicinal plants, bushmeat and plantains.

With him were three wrestlers—men with sculpted bodies and bulging muscles similar to security agents in the 22nd century. Biték's father asked his wife to cook the bushmeat with the plantains.

As the sun rose, Biték's father entered his son's room, woke him up and asked him to follow him to the backyard. Biték followed. When he arrived, he saw the fire burning. He took a closer look into the fire and saw the reddened knife. On the other side, he saw his mother and his father's other two wives cleaning the bushmeat. Suddenly, he was surrounded by the three strongmen, so he asked his father what was going on.

'Biték, today you will be circumcised', replied his father.

'Dad, why didn't you tell me I'd be circumcised today. I should have prepared', Biték told his father.

Biték's father let out a chuckle and replied, 'I asked my father the same question, and he told me, "Does the panther warn his prey? Like death that strikes without warning, the panther attacks its prey. You must be ready for the panther. Life is unpredictable. Death is the only certainty. When death strikes, you must be ready. Birth is not the *beginning of life but death. Life is the preparation for death. You must be ready when death comes.'''*

The fire with the circumcision knife was still burning while Biték and his father were talking. Biték began trembling—his whole body wet with sweat falling like drops of water.

'Is the knife in the fire for my circumcision?' Biték asked his father.

'Yes', the man replied.

'Don't you have any remorse about inflicting that much pain on me?' Biték retorted.

'No remorse, my son', replied his father. *'This is life's lesson, and the greatest lessons are learned in pain. The more painful it is, the bigger the lesson.'*

'Isn't there any other way to learn this life lesson without slicing a part of my penis?' Biték asked, his voice cracking and tears running down his face.

'Circumcision is the heritage of our ancestors from the Nile Valley in Egypt. Therefore, it is not about cutting off the piece of flesh that covers your manhood but rather about showing loyalty to ancestors and reaffirming your belonging to Saa, the most ancient of ancients', replied his father.

The man continued,

'No man in this village will give his daughter in marriage to a man that does not show loyalty to our tradition and ancestors.'

Biték was so afraid to be circumcised to the extent that he was ready to give up marriage altogether, questioning his father about its importance.

'Birth, marriage and death are the most important events in a person's life. Although these are common to all peoples of the world, they are received differently by each one. Marriage is the line of resistance of our people. It allows us to reproduce the human species not only in quantity but also in quality. However, marriage is held to reproduce not only human species but also knowledge and tradition and ensure the survival of our tribe', Biték's father replied.

'How can we preserve tradition and pass it on to future generations without marriage? We have to protect and pass this on. It is imperative for all those concerned with the future of our people and humanity.'

Then, Biték asked, *'Can we avoid my circumcision?'*

'*I asked my father the same question*', replied his father, '*And this was my father's response.*

"*The people of the rock practice circumcision from generation to generation. Your birth among the people of the rock condemns you to such. Circumcision is part of our tradition. Can one avoid tradition? Yes, but at the expense of one's life."*'

'*I thought tradition is good and not supposed to kill*', Biték asked his father.

'*Tradition is beyond good and bad. Tradition does not kill; it is the understanding of the universe. What kills is the violation of tradition and its laws and rites, that is, the laws of the universe*', replied his father, who continued, saying, '*Tradition is also our social contract. Our ancestors signed the constitution ratified by Hilolombi, the most ancient of ancients and supreme divinity.*

As in any country, the constitution must be respected; it guarantees the good of the people, may it be prosperity, peace and development. Like anywhere else, it is a crime to violate the constitution.

The constitution commits those who signed it and those who did not, and engages future generations.

Long before we were born, our ancestors engaged us to this constitution. By signing this social contract, they committed themselves, their ancestors, Hilolombi, ourselves and our descendants. We are because our ancestors were. We are the continuity of our ancestors; we are our ancestors, so we are the ones who signed this constitution. Our misfortune is that we don't honour our commitments. A man is his words. Come hell or high water, your yes must be yes, and your no must be no.'

After saying this, Biték's father ordered the three men to secure Biték so that he could not move. While they were getting a hold of Biték, his father walked towards the fire, took the reddened knife and went back to the frightened Biték who asked to be blindfolded, as he did not dare see his manhood cut. His request was rejected by his father, who said,

'Circumcision is also about courage. Courage is not the absence of fear but its mastery and control. At your birth, Gambi, the oracle, said that you would save the Ndog Mbog Village from the hands of its enemies. How can you do that without courage?'

His father continued,

'Slavery is our greatest tragedy, and this would not have been possible without the direct participation

of our people. Today, the German invasion repeats the tragic past of Africans' direct participation in the destruction of Africa. Never forget this. Your greatest pains in life will be inflicted upon you by those for whom you have the greatest love. That is why I, your father, will personally circumcise you.'

After saying this, Biték's father grabbed Biték's shaft and cut off the skin that covered it. Biték continuously screamed like a cow being slaughtered. His blood spilled and covered everyone around him. To clean the mess, his father gathered some plants and cleaned his wound. Biték had a soft, new loincloth that had been sewn only for his circumcision, and he must stay covered with it until the wound heals.

The village went to Biték's house to celebrate this milestone. Parents arrived with their daughters and paraded them in front of Biték, telling him that he could already get married now that he was circumcised. The bushmeat was served, and people ate, drank palm wine and danced.

CHAPTER 4
BITÉK AND THE CHIEF'S SECOND WIFE

Biték was now a grown-up man who has mastered fishing, hunting and farming. He was ravishing, making him a lover of women. However, his eyes were set on only one woman — Kindap, one of the two wives of the Ndog Mbog village chief.

Kindap was a woman of sophisticated beauty and secretly the apple of Biték's eye. Being the chief's wife, she was hard to approach. Thus, like a leopard waiting for the right moment to pounce on its prey, Biték would cautiously go after his alluring target.

Saturday was market day, and farmers, fishers and hunters visited the marketplace to sell products. In this location, Biték proved to be as good a woman hunter as he is an animal one.

One Saturday in 1914, Kindap decided to go to the marketplace by herself to get bushmeat — something out of the ordinary. Although known for his hunting skills, Biték was also famous for having the best bushmeat in the area. Thus, upon her arrival at the marketplace, she headed directly to Biték's stall. This was the perfect opportunity for Biték to chat up the chief's second wife.

Kindap: *How much is your bushmeat?*

Biték: *Do name your price, Your Majesty.*

Kindap: *I have five francs.*

Biték: *No, Your Majesty. I am asking about your actual price.*

Kindap: *Are five francs not enough for your bushmeat? Who else will give you five francs? I am not giving more than that.*

Biték: *Forgive me for upsetting you, Your Majesty. I am not asking about what Your Majesty must pay for my bushmeat. My bushmeat and I* *belong to Your Majesty, and she can do whatever she pleases with us. I am asking about the price for our village's goddess to listen and grant me the desire of my heart.*

Kindap: *The desire in any farmer's heart is fertile land and plenty of rain to water the seed for a good harvest. Meanwhile, the desire in any hunter's heart is to kill animals each time he goes hunting by either setting traps in the bushes or other means. That is all I know. How can I grant the desire of your heart?*

Biték: *Killing animals and selling them have never fulfilled the desires of any hunter's heart, apart from putting food on the table. Your Majesty does not see a fellow human being; the only thing she sees is a hunter. Before a hunter, I am first a human being with flesh, bones and a beating heart. Hunters, fishers, farmers, chiefs and Mbombogs — we all have hearts, and love is the only desire of any man's heart.*

Kindap: *Prayer and righteousness are needed for the goddess to listen and grant you whatever your heart longs for.*

Biték: *Today, I think our gods have heard my prayers and come to grant me my heart's desire. Knock, and it shall be opened to you; seek, and you shall find; and ask, and it shall be given.*

Kindap: *Yes. The gods have come and heard your prayers, but our gods are the gods of Maa, righteousness, justice, truth and wisdom. They will never give unto you what would lead to your death. They will never open a door that would lead to your demise. And they will never provide you what belongs to somebody else. Here are five francs for your bushmeat; I am not paying more than that. Say no more.*

Although Biték spoke in parables, Kindap was far from being simpleminded as the chief's second wife. She perfectly understood what Biték was doing. However, she was amazed and impressed with Biték's courage to do what he did. No one has ever done that to the chief's wife, as doing so would mean suicide.

The next Saturday, Biték did not sell but was merely hiding in the marketplace to see if Kindap would return. Biték reassured himself that if the woman comes back, it would mean that she is interested in him. As Biték anticipated, Kindap returned to the marketplace. From his location, he could see her keeping an eye out for him.

Kindap returned again to the marketplace the following Saturday. This time, Biték was selling.

Kindap: *How much is your bushmeat today?*

Bitēk: *I have already told Your Majesty that my bushmeat and I belong to her, so she can do whatever she pleases with us.*

Kindap: *For your safety, I beg you to leave me alone. A female monkey once said to her child, 'Be very careful while jumping from branch to branch. All branches are not dried and strong enough, and never forget that humans have set up deadly traps on the ground.' The young monkey failed to listen to his mother, and while performing hazardous fits, he held onto a brittle branch that broke and found himself trapped on the ground. Looking at him helplessly, his mother said to him, 'Didn't I warn you? The incredulous returns from the hill of stubborn people with a swinging penis.'*

Bitēk: *If Your Majesty wanted to be left alone, she would not have come here today. She would have sent one of her servants. Last Saturday, I saw Your Majesty looking for me in the marketplace.*

Kindap: *Don't you know that it is against our tradition to take someone else's wife? More so, a chief's wife. Are you not afraid of death?*

Bitēk: *Death is the shadow of life. Can we run away from our shadow? It follows us everywhere, and* so does death. One day, we will all eventually die. Today, tomorrow, in a hundred years — it does not matter. What matters is living a happy life before we pass away. So, I prefer to be joyful for a minute with Your Majesty and die the minute after than to live a hundred years without a minute of happiness. Is Your Majesty happy?

Kindap: *You have just killed a female lion. Indeed, you are the greatest hunter of the Ndog Mbog village. Here are five francs for your bushmeat.*

Biték: *No, Your Majesty. Would you do me the favour of taking my bushmeat as a present from me?*

Kindap: *If only you stop calling me 'Your Majesty'. You can call me Kindap. We are friends now.*

This is how Kindap, the second wife of the Ndog Mbog village chief, fell in love with the hunter Biték.

Chapter 5
BITÉK ESCAPES NDOG MBOG VILLAGE

Each of the chief's wives had her bedroom. As a way of avoiding jealousy between the two women, the chief made it a point not to spend consecutive nights with either wife, alternating between them. With this set-up, Kindap knew precisely when the chief would be spending the night with her and when he would not.

Kindap's heart now beats for Biték. She could no longer live without him. Without Biték by her side, her life was meaningless, as he became her life's purpose. However, she was the chief's wife and could not see Biték as much as her heart desired. Kindap could only see him on Saturdays at the marketplace, which she did the following weekend.

Kindap: *I have to wait for a whole week to see you again. A week has become an eternity to me. Day and night, my heart longs for you. Satisfy my soul, wipe the tears in my eyes and put joy in my heart and a smile on my lips. I beg you to come and be with me tonight.*

Biték: *During my birth, Mbombog Som prophesied that long I shall live and I am the man from whom death ran. Is tonight the end of my life at the chief's house? The words of our gods shall always come to pass. My body, heart and soul belong to you, and if I must live, it is to satisfy your heart's desires, no matter the danger it presents. I prefer to live a day as a lion and in happiness than a hundred years as a sheep and in sadness.*

Kindap: *There is nothing to worry about. The chief will spend the night with his first wife, so tonight would not be the end of your life but its joyous beginning. I will make tonight the happiest of all your nights.*

Around midnight, Biték snuck into the chief's house where Kindap was waiting for him.

They headed to the woman's bedroom and made love. Afterwards, Kindap spoke to Biték.

Kindap: *I never removed my clothes for a man; the chief has always been the one to do so. But tonight, with joy, I stripped off my clothing for you. I never gave my virginity to a man. The chief took it by force. He has power and rules over our land. But tonight, with glee, I gave you what was taken by force. The chief rules over our land, but you rule over my heart. In my heart, the chief has become the hunter, who has then become the chief. I am your servant, and the only wage I demand from you is love. All these years at the chief's house, I lived a lie. I smiled because I had to. Tonight, for the first time, a man made me smile, and that man is you. You made me understand what happiness is. You took me where no man has taken me. Only death shall separate me from you. I no longer want to live a lie. I beg you. Let us run away and never return to this village.*

Biték: *Run away and go where? The chief will find and kill us.*

Kindap: *Sooner or later, they will find out anyway and kill us. Let us run away now before they do.*

Biték: *I think I should leave now, while it is still dark outside.*

After that night, Biték would regularly sneak into the chief's house to make love with Kindap, and each Saturday, Kindap would visit the marketplace to buy bushmeat from Biték. One day, Kindap finally convinced Biték to run away with her from the village. However, before doing so, Biték visited Kindap again at the chief's house, which had become a regular event, only to be caught by the chief as he was making love to her. Even though the chief slept in Kindap's bedroom the night before, they were unaware that the chief fought with his first wife, prompting him to sleep at his second wife's bedroom for the night. It was the survival of the fittest. Biték pushed the chief and ran away.

The chief took the traditional drum immediately and started beating it to call his people. The entire village awoke to the sound of the drum and gathered at the chief's house.

The chief announced that he had caught Biték sleeping with his second wife. Following tradition, this was considered a transgression. Therefore, Biték must die. To this, Mbombog Som responded,

'Before climbing a tree, one should make sure that his underwear is clean. While eating the palm of the Shimpaze's hand, look at your own. I am the

Mbombog, which means I am the traditional chief. Therefore, nobody knows traditional laws better than I do. It is against our tradition to sleep with someone else's wife and kill unless done in self-defence. As such, Biték shall be brought alive and punished accordingly.'

The chief replied,

'I am the chief, and I order the death of Biték.'

To this, Mbombog Som said,

'Who made you chief? You were made chief by the same Germans who overthrew our tradition. Similar to them, you rule by the law of arms, not by tradition. This is our ancestors' land and must be governed by the ancestral law, which is tradition. In this village, as a Mbombog, I am its custodian. Our ancestors enthroned me.'

The chief replied,

'What gives you the right to deny my authority? I'll inform the Germans of the rebellion you're planning. My words are final. I want Biték *dead. Search each house in the village. Catch him before he leaves, kill him and bring me his dead body. Then, I will offer him as food to my leopards.'*

Then, Mbombog Som said,

'I am not planning a rebellion. However, I must speak the truth. I have remained silent for so many years, but I am now too old. The soul belongs to ancestors, and the body belongs to the world. Your leopards will eat tonight according to Biték's destiny.'

Upon saying this, Mbombog Som left the chief's house.

That night, the hunter Biték became the hunted. The villagers were armed with petrol lamps, machetes and spears, all chanting that he must die. Biték sought refuge at his female cousin's house, where he hid under her bed.

Apart from their ability to consult all-knowing ancestors, Ba Mbombog or traditional priests are always in contact with marine spirits, describing the latter as beings of extreme and incomparable beauty. However, this level of beauty was possessed by Biték's cousin, causing people to refer to her as the marine spirit of the Ndog Mbog village.

Aside from her allure, she was as tall as a papaya tree, with firm breasts as round as oranges and as soft as pillows that can sway the hardest of hearts. She had a voice as pure as melody, skin as smooth as a cocoyam leaf that captures the colours of darkness, a gaze as innocent as that of a newborn and teeth whiter than snow. With her long hair in dreadlocks, her smile was as beautiful as a butterfly taking flight, making every knee bend. She walked as graceful as a gazelle, with birds as her companions. Her presence exuded the feeling of basking under the shade of a baobab tree. It was even said that her sight alone drove men to their physical limits.

As such, when the armed villagers arrived at her house, they could not help but be blown away by the woman before their eyes. To add fuel to the lovely fire, they found her dressed seductively. She had an alluring vibe as she answered the villagers, saying she saw Biték running away towards Ngambe, the village where his mother was from. Upon hearing this, the villagers did not even stop to search her house and proceeded to find Biték before he escapes entirely.

Biték's cousin also played the charming card with the chief. She dressed in sultry clothing and ran to the chief, telling him that she saw Biték running towards Ngambe. In response, the chief ordered all villagers to run in that direction to catch Biték and kill him before reaching his mother's village.

Biték's cousin then returned to her house, where Biték was still hiding under the bed. She told him, *'You can come out now.'*

According to tradition, those who eat a cat's head do not die in a foreign land. They will always return to die in the land of their ancestors. So, Biték's cousin offered one of her cats as a sacrifice so that Biték would not die in exile. That same night, she asked Biték to catch one of her cats and kill it. *'The clock is not on our side; we have less than an hour to kill, cook and eat it'*, she said.

Before killing the cat, Biték asked it to forgive him, as tradition requires before any sacrifice. Mbog is an ancestral religion based on respect and knowledge of the universe. Because animals are part of the universe, they equally have the right to life as humans, and some animals symbolise divinities.

Biték's cousin entered her kitchen and took a cooking stone traditionally used to blend ingredients. She spoke to the cooking stone with these words.

'You were a cooking stone. Now, you are the rocky mountain, the holy cave, the almighty power of

the supreme divinity and the most ancient of ancients, Hilolombi.'

Then, she took a Mbongoo seed and added it to the cooking stone, saying,

'I blend you on this stone so that you may give to all those who eat you the strength of the rock.'

Biték's cousin quickly cooked the cat in a traditional black sauce known as Mbongoo, a traditional delicacy. However, not all ingredients were available to give the Mbongoo sauce its usual and delicious taste. In under 30 minutes of cooking, Biték's cousin served the cat's head to Biték, saying, *'This is not supposed to be tasty as it is a remedy. Not any cuisine.'*

After eating, Biték's cousin told him,

'I tricked them into thinking you're going towards Ngambe, so you must head towards the opposite direction and leave this village before the sun rises.'

Biték hugged and thanked his cousin and said to her,

'Perhaps I will never see my brothers and sisters again, but I will always remember you. Do not worry about me.'

With the help of his cousin, Biték successfully ran away from the Ndog Mbog village.

CHAPTER 6

THE INITIATION OF MBOMBOG NDJAMI

Africa was colonised, and no area of African life was spared from colonialism. Africans' way of life, dominant religions, official languages, institutions and thoughts were muddled by colonisation.

To weaken and passively colonise African people, colonisers had to alienate Africans, meaning they had to completely uproot them from their values and principles and impose upon them imported virtues.

Thus, as a result of foreign invasion, African religions, spiritual beliefs and traditions were banned, and Africans were converted by force and arms to new religions, which, ironically, are nothing but deformations and plagiarisms of ancient African traditions.

German colonisers overthrew the Ngok Lituba society's traditional organization wherein the traditional chiefs and rulers were Mbombogs and replaced them with village chiefs to serve their colonialist interests. They also attributed the title of traditional chiefs to these village leaders, although they did not govern according to ancestral and traditional laws but rather the unfair laws established by colonisers. These village chiefs ruled with iron fists, and decisions on the right to life and death were passed on to them by colonisers.

In the Ndog Mbog village, Mbog, the ancestral tradition and religion, was banished by German colonisers. In the same vein, the Mbombogs or patriarchs were persecuted.

This persecution resulted in three groups of Mbombogs. One radical group refused to convert to Christianity at the peril of their lives. They were persecuted, killed or forced into exile and solitude in the remote depths of the forest. The second group of Mbombogs abdicated their responsibility by abandoning tradition and converting to Christianity. Then, the third group of Mbombogs pretended to be converted to avoid persecution but were not, in reality, to protect tradition, for one had to stay alive to conserve and pass on the tradition to the next generation.

Mbombog Som was one of those who pretended to have been converted to Christianity to avoid persecution. However, he was unmasked by his frankness to the village chief about Biték.

Although Mbombog Som had never been involved in colonial affairs, following his altercation with the chief over Biték, he was labelled as a dissident to the German colonial power.

Mbombog Som understood that, as promised by the chief, correspondence would be sent to the German colonial administration, which would cost him prison, at the very least, or worse, death.

Therefore, that night, Mbombog Som left the chief's residence with full knowledge of the consequences lying ahead and went home. He had a son named Ndjami, with whom he shared what had happened at the chief's residence. He said to him, *'Tonight, I will pass on the tradition. I will enthrone you as Mbombog because, in the days that follow, I risk being arrested for rebellion for contradicting the chief.'*

That same night, nine Mbombogs met at a secret meeting at the tomb of Makani, Mbombog Som's father, to pass on the tradition to Ndjami.

In the presence of nine Mbombogs, Mbombog Som took his son Ndjami naked to Makani's grave. Mbombog Som struck his staff thrice on the tomb, poured a small amount of palm wine on his father's grave, symbolism expressing gratitude to his father and said,

'Dad, it is me, your son, Mbombog Som Makani. I am here with other Mbombogs. Dad, in the same way that you passed on the tradition to me, I have also come to pass on the tradition to your grandson Djami Som.'

While Djami was naked on his grandfather's grave, his father, Mbombog Som, dressed in traditional attire, holding a traditional broom known as Jai li Mbog, and spoke to him, saying,

'Unable to answer existential questions and convince us rationally, methodically and philosophically on metaphysical issues, colonisers have destroyed the table of philosophical dialogue.

Unable to convince us, their only option was to replace thought with weapons and wisdom with war, and impose upon us their bloodthirsty theologies and sterile understanding of the universe.

They tell us about revelations God has given them and seek to impose these revelations on people to whom God has not given them. At the same time, they tell us that God is omnipresent. If so, it means that He is everywhere, so there is no need to convert others. A universal God means He is also in our tradition. If their God is not in our tradition as they claim, it means their God is not omnipresent.

An omnipresent God also means that He gives revelations and speaks to all peoples of the Earth. As such, there is no need to convert others. God speaks to us through our ancestors. How were our ancestors able to build pyramids and align them with stars if God did not talk to them? How were our ancestors able to discover science if God did not speak to them?

God is the universe, and the universe is God. Each and everything is a part of the universe. Each and everything is within the universe, and nothing is outside it. Our ancestors are our mediators between the visible and the invisible. Day and night, the universe speaks to us. We are all equally children of the universe.

Those who do not respect the universe or wage wars can neither speak nor teach about God to others.

The natural order of things has been altered; tradition no longer rules. It is banished, and its patriarchs have become fugitives. Do not be a fugitive; a patriarch does not abandon his throne.

By day, you will go to their churches, and by night, you will visit the sanctuaries of your ancestors.

By day, you will bow before their gods, and by night, you will bow before the gods of your ancestors.

By day, you will speak of their prophets, and by night, you will talk of your ancestors.

By day, you shall take communion, and by night, you shall have kola nuts.

By day, you shall baptise your children in their churches, and by night, you shall bathe them with Mabui and bless them on their ancestors' graves.

By day, you shall carry the Bible, and by night, you shall carry Mbot i Mbog.

By day, you shall visit Jerusalem, and by night, you shall visit Ngok Lituba.

Our language is the most remarkable heritage I have received from our ancestors. This same language is the most precious thing I pass on to you. Language is the fundamental guardian of tradition; it carries the knowledge of the universe.

Behind every word lies a universe of infinite knowledge — a force that creates, transforms and destroys. Our language is the gateway to the wisdom and secrets of the universe.

Even if Mbombogs were to disappear, language would transmit tradition and initiate new Mbombogs.

It is the spoken word that awakens Mabui. It is the spoken word that revives Bi Mban Bi Mbog. It is the spoken word that gives power to Jai Li Mbog. It is the spoken word that provides power to Tongo.

During the day, you will speak the language of the coloniser to your children, and at night, you will talk to them in the language of their ancestors.

You shall stray away from colonial affairs and politics. By doing so, you will stay alive to protect and pass on the tradition to the future generation. By wisdom, the turtle protected his mother from a hungry lion, and the colonisers are the hungry lions thirsty for blood.

Never allow your mind to be captivated by constipated and sterile theologies, and never reject our tradition. To know is to live, and to ignore is to pass by life and die before dying. If knowledge is our right, responsibility is our duty. In terms of origins, make your tradition a point of honour and pass it on to future generations because it is the only thing that is ours — our language and tradition.

For future generations whose brains will be shaped by colonialism, Mbog (tradition) will be nothing but evil. However, no matter how long it takes, our tradition, buried in the deepest depths of the Earth by colonisers, will be exhumed.

You are the witness who will have to answer to future generations born in an upside-down world.

You must give an account to future generations born in the land of their ancestors and who, instead of speaking their ancestors' language, will use the language of its executioners.

You will tell narratives to future generations born in the land of their ancestors without knowing them but would know the ancestors of executioners.

You will also pass on the story to future generations born in the land of their ancestors but *despise the gods of their ancestors and worship the gods of executioners.'*

Mbombog Som and the nine Mbombogs present that night bathed Ndjami in a traditional bath on his grandfather's grave. He then locked foreheads with his son, chewed a kola nut and spat it on his son's face. The man also drank a few gulps of palm wine and spat it again. Then, he gave a Don seed to his son and asked him to eat it.

Each of the nine Mbombogs present that night also did the same. They locked foreheads with Ndjami. They also drank few throats of palm wine and spat it on the kid's face again. Ndjami also ate a Don seed from each of the nine Mbombogs.

Mbombog Som eulogised the universe.

'Mbog eeh!'

'Mbog eeh!'

'Mbog eeh!'

Then, the nine Mbombogs responded *'Sai'* to each salutation.

Holding the symbol of power and the visible world called Jai Li Mbog firmly in his hand, Mbombog Som asked Ndjami to grab Jai Li Mbog. Still naked on his grandfather's grave, Ndjami grabbed the Jai Li Mbog out of his father's hand with all his might. Mbombog Som, who also firmly held the staff, asked his son to grab too. Ndjami did so again.

Mbombog Som gave Ndjami the traditional bag containing the traditional relics handed down from one patriarch to another and said to him,

'From now on, you are Mbombog. This bag is evidence that you are now the custodian of tradition.' He added, *'Are there any objections?'*

To this, the nine Mbombogs present replied, *'There is no objection at all.'* Then, Mbombog Som said to his son, *'Neither ancestors nor the living opposes your enthronement.'*

This is how Ndjami was secretly enthroned as Mbombog. As advised by his father, he pretended to convert to Christianity by joining the Presbyterian Church, where he became a church elder. His father, Mbombog Som, was placed under house arrest by the German colonial administration until his death.

CHAPTER 7
BITÉK STARTS ANEW IN PORT HARCOURT

Biték climbed hills and ran across the Babimbi forest laden with leopards. In the middle of the night, Biték arrived at the Nsas Nanga River. No boat was available to cross it, and Biték could not afford to wait until dawn. He had no choice but to swim.

Nsas Nanga was named after the son of Nge Nanga Nanga, who led some Basaa people from the Lake Chad to Nigeria. In honour of Nge Nanga Nanga, some Basaa people of Nigeria called themselves Bassa-Nge. Nge Nanga Nanga entered with another group of Basaa in northern

Cameroon and then in Southern Cameroon. Nsas, Nge and Nanga are also gods in the mythology of the Basaa and Ngok Lituba people.

Before jumping into the water, Biték prayed to Nsas Nanga.

'Nsas Nanga, I, Biték, son of Bimai, do not deserve to be carried by you.

I have transgressed against tradition.

My hands are full of blood, and all my life, I have been a hunter.

I am malicious.

If, by your grace and mercy, you carry me across the shore,

never again will I be a hunter. Never again shall blood be in my hands and malice be in my heart.'

After his prayer to Nsas Nanga, Biték courageously jumped into the river and started swimming. Biték saw a slab of wood floating on the water. Exhausted from swimming, he decided to sit on the wood and let it carry him across the shore to a place called Bikok. When Biték arrived, he realised that what he thought had been a piece of wood was, in reality, a massive snake.

After only a few days, Biték walked a distance measuring around 100 kilometres and reached Douala, the economic capital of Cameroon. Although the Ndog Mbog village chief has no authority outside his area, Biték still felt unsafe in Cameroon. Thus, he carried on his journey and reached the southwest region. From there, he took a boat to neighbouring Nigeria. He continued his journey to Southern Nigeria, and in 1915, Biték arrived at the Nigerian city of Port Harcourt.

Biték's full name was Biték bi Bimai, which means 'Biték, son of Bimai.' Upon his arrival in Port Harcourt, he changed his name to B.B Cameroon. B.B were initials of both of his names, Biték and Bimai, and Cameroon was the country he hailed from. Biték wanted to have a name that sounded English because Britain occupied the land he was in.

Although Biték changed his name, he could not speak English and local Nigerian languages, which was one of the challenges he had to overcome in Port Harcourt. He slept on the streets and lived from the generosity of passers-by.

Luckily, Biték was introduced to a British man named Scott, who needed a domestic worker. Biték eventually became Mr. Scott's doorman and gardener, and through this job, he met Amadi, a female domestic worker. Amadi's responsibilities for Mr. Scott included doing the laundry, cooking his food and keeping his house clean.

Amadi was from the Igbo tribe, and she was stunning. On his first day at work, Biték saw Amadi and fancied her immediately. Biték hardly focused on his work, as he was always distracted by the beautiful woman's presence. However, he was reluctant to express his feelings as what happened with Kindap was still fresh in his memory. He barely spoke English as well. As such, his eyes were always locked on Amadi, and his lips had a hint of charm.

With all these, Amadi could sense that Biték wanted to tell her something, but he lacked the courage to speak his mind. On the other hand, it looked like Amadi also wanted Biték to approach her, but he remained silent. Each time Amadi turned her back, she would find Biték looking at her, and vice versa.

Biték was a foreigner in Port Harcourt. He knew nothing about the customs and traditions of the Igbo people and the things he could and could not do. Thus, he had to be as careful as possible. He could lose his job for flirting with Amadi, or worse, the Igbo people could kill him. Biték was a hunter, and for him, hunting animals was no different from seducing women. In both cases, one must only be patient and jump on the prey at the right moment.

One scorching afternoon, Amadi, who looked more tired than usual, was doing Mr. Scott's laundry. Biték noticed this and approached Amadi.

Biték: *Please let me wash Mr. Scott's clothes. You can dry them instead.*

Amadi: *Thank you very much, but I will be fine.*

Biték: *Please let me help you. My heart gets wounded each time I see a beautiful woman such as you burning under the sun.*

Amadi: *The sun does not burn black people. Black people are the sun. Didn't you know that? Be aware that my heart is an infertile land, and no seed, not even the seed of love, can grow here.*

Biték: *I am the farmer of love, and there is no land, place or object on Earth where the seed of love* *does not grow; it even grows in the Sahara and on the rocks. Hundreds of times I have planted the seed of love, and hundreds of times it had grown. Like the wind that blows wherever it wills, the seed of love also grows wherever it wishes. Love is the only seed that grows on the four elements: earth, water, air and fire. Love blooms where it is least expected. Just let me sow the seed of love.*

Amadi: *Are you flirting with me, or do you want to help me do the laundry?*

Biték put a charming and irresistible smile on his face, and Amadi finally accepted his help, doing the laundry together. They even played around with water, as how kids would, and without Amadi realising, the seed of love began sprouting in her heart. To thank Biték for helping her, Amadi brought some food for him the next day.

Amadi: *I brought you something to eat for having helped me yesterday.*

Biték: *Thank you very much. Blessed is he who gives. What do you call this food?*

Amadi: *It is pounded yam and egusi soup, my people's favourite food. For us Igbo people, yam is sacred. It was given to us by Chukwu, our most* *powerful spirit. Each year, across Igboland, we celebrate Iri Ji Ohuru, the Yam Festival. Eri, father of Nri, and Nnamaku, his wife, were sent by Chukwu, a sky god. When Eri came down from the sky, he had to stand on an ant heap, as all land was then a morass. He complained to Chukwu, who thereupon sent him an Awka blacksmith to dry up the land. While Eri was alive, he and his dependents were fed by Chukwu, and their food was AzuIgwe, which is fish from heaven. When Eri died, this food supply ceased. Nri complained to Chukwu but was told that to get food, he would have to kill and bury his eldest son and daughter. When Nri objected, Chukwu promised to send Dioka from the sky to carve the ichi or facial cicatrisation marks on the two children's foreheads. After Dioka arrived and engraved the ichi on the faces of the two children, Nri slit their throats and buried them in separate graves. Twelve days later, shoots appeared from their graves. From his son's grave, Nri dug up yam. He cooked and ate it, and he found it so pleasing that he fell into a sleep so deep his family thought he was dead. When he awoke, he told his astonished family what he had done. The next day, Nri dug up cocoyam from his daughter's grave, ate them and, likewise, slept again. Therefore, yam is called 'son of Nri,' and cocoyam, 'daughter of Nri.' To this day, the firstborn son and daughter of Nri are marked with the ichi to commemorate the miracle.*

Chukwu had ordered Nri to distribute yams, cocoyam and other goods to all the people in Igboland.

Biték: *According to your people's tradition, yam is considered sacred. But what does your tradition say about marriage? Are Igbo women allowed to marry foreigners? I am asking because my heart has been longing for you day and night since I arrived at our master's house.*

Amadi: *Yes, according to our tradition, an Igbo woman can marry a foreigner. The only crime is taking an Igbo woman without doing the wedding rites, which also includes the bride price.*

Biték and Amadi then embraced and gave each other kisses. He proposed to Amadi, who then accepted. Biték paid the bride price, and Amadi became his wife. For 15 years, Biték continued to work for Mr. Scott. With 2 male children, the couple also lived together for 15 years.

Indeed, there is no land where the seed of love does not grow. Biték had sown the seed of love in Amadi's heart, where it blossomed and grew into a big tree that bore plenty of fruits of bliss that Amadi could no longer do without, and for which she cursed the gods of her people and was even willing to sacrifice her life.

CHAPTER 8

BITÉK'S FATE AT THE YAM FESTIVAL

One night in 1933, the Igbo elders of Port Harcourt gathered to prepare for the annual Yam Festival. Amadi's older brother was among them. He was joined by Di Ji, the expert yam cultivator in the community, and Oji Ofo, the recognised ritual head of the Yam Festival.

Oji Ofo stood and opened the meeting by reciting the Yam Prayer.

'New Yam of this year, we are cutting you today.

We are slicing you into four pieces.

We have seen how whitish you are.

The yam deity, run. Come.

Bless this yam, and may one tuber become four

in each of our barns.

Ancestors, behold the new yam, share the feast with us.

Haa! Amin!'

After the prayer, Di Ji stood and addressed the assembly, saying,

'Chukwu, our sky God, has sent plenty of rain this year all over Igboland.

There was no infertile inch of land all over the land this year.

There was no tuber of yam planted that has not flourished this year.

Indeed, each tuber of yam has become four.

The harvest of yam this year was plenty, but few were sons and daughters of Igboland.

This year, no Igbo family will sleep hungry.

May Chukwu, our God, be praised.'

After this, Oji Ofo stood again and addressed the assembly.

'Dear brothers, you know how much yam is sacred to us. During the famine, yam was given to us by our gods. Nri, our ancestor, sacrificed his two children to receive yam from Chukwu, our Sky God. Then, he dug up yam from his son's grave. Yam was also the reincarnation of the first son of an Afikpo woman sacrificed following the oracle's orders. To receive yam in our land, we must sacrifice to please the spirits, and this has been the custom of our people from generation to generation. For this year's Yam Festival, the oracles have chosen B.B Cameroon as the sacrifice. We will arrest and kill him the night before the festival, and his blood shall be offered to Chukwu in the Ukwu-Egbu tree. We will cook and eat his body with yams.'

After the gathering, Amadi's older brother, who was present at the meeting, ran to inform his sister Amadi that B.B Cameroon, her husband, will be eaten at the Yam Festival. Upon hearing this, Amadi started crying and cursed the tradition of her people, saying,

'Chukwu, our most powerful spirit, how cruel are you? Just because of yam, you want to take the only man who has brought sunshine to my life. Chukwu, I will never let you take my happiness away. Chukwu, *you will never make me a widow. Chukwu, I curse you. I curse the Igbo people!'*

Biték held his wife to console her.

Biték: *Before marrying you, didn't I pay the bride price to the Igbo people? Didn't I observe the laws and traditions of your people? Death is not my portion. At my birth, Mbombog, the traditional priest of my people, said that long I must live and I am the man from whom death ran away. So many times, death will run away from me. I will see my grandchildren and save my village. When I was young, I survived the Germans' Mbandi Attack. I also escaped from death when I slept with one of the wives of my village's chief. And I will also escape from death in Igboland. Amadi, alive shall I return to my country.*

Amadi: *I cannot live without you. Please take me with you.*

Biték: *If I take you with me, they will know that your older brother betrayed them and kill him.*

Amadi: *He must die. Yam is the food of men, and each year, at the Yam Festival, my brother eats innocent people. Let every person receive what is due to him. May he who kills another go with the dead. May evil be met with evil. May good be followed by good.*

Chapter 9
BITÉK FLEES FROM PORT HARCOURT

The next morning, Biték and Amadi, accompanied by their two male children, ran to Mr. Scott and informed him they were quitting their job as they had to flee to Cameroon. Surprised, Mr. Scott could not understand why his most loyal workers were suddenly leaving. He asked for more information and why they were running to Cameroon. Biték explained that he was chosen as a sacrifice by the oracles for the annual Yam Festival. Mr. Scott responded,

'If that is the case, there is no way you can escape. They must have been following you from the day their oracles have chosen you. If you try to run away, they

will catch you. Run away or stay; they are still going to catch you. You and Amadi have been truly loyal to me, and as compensation, I will help you go to Cameroon.'

With his Land Rover, Mr. Scott and his armed bodyguards drove Biték and his family to the Nigeria–Cameroon border, where Biték and his family could board a boat to Cameroon. Throughout the journey, Biték was hidden inside the trunk of Mr. Scott's car. As a protective measure, Mr. Scott ordered his bodyguards to shoot whoever stops them and searches the vehicle. After some time, they safely arrived at the border.

There, Biték surprisingly announced to Amadi and his children that he would not take them to Cameroon. Amadi started crying.

Amadi: *Why, why, why? I cannot live without you. You are not going without us.*

Biték: *I promise I will return and get you and the children.*

Amadi: *The Igbo people will kill me. Take us with you.*

Biték: *No. It is your brother who will be killed. I will come and get you and the children.*

However, Biték knew that he would never return to Nigeria and see his family again. As such, Biték told his children,

'Never forget where your father comes from. Your father is your head, and your mother is your tail. If you forget your father, you will lose yourself in the wildness of life. And if you forget your mother, you will have no strength. Even if you know the path of life, you will never reach your destination with no strength to walk the walk. Then, if you have strength without knowledge of the way, that strength is powerless and useless. Never kill and take someone else's wife. Transgression leads to death. With righteousness, you will jump over the highest wall, swim the most dangerous water and cross the largest desert. He who runs in every man perishes his life, just as the soul that runs in all souls perishes its spirit.'

To each of his children, Biték gave a piece of paper where he wrote the names of his ancestors and village. Then, he said to them,

'Listen carefully.

We are the continuity of our ancestors.

Our ancestors and we are one.

This is a link we cannot destroy.

One who curses his ancestors curses himself.

One who blesses his ancestors blesses himself.

You curse the Igbo people, you curse yourself.

You bless the Igbo people, you bless yourself.

You curse Chukwu, you curse yourself.

You bless Chukwu, you bless yourself.

We are like trees, and tradition is our roots.

You cut your roots, and you die.

Dead people are not dead.

Ancestors are the living dead.

Ancestors are the eyes of the living.

One who rejects his tradition blinds himself.

Only a fool pierces his eyes.

Ancestors are never hungry, so they never eat.

Ancestors do not eat their progeny.

Instead, ancestors feed them.

Ancestors are hungry only when tradition is in the hands of cannibals.

In Igboland, tradition is in the hands of cannibals.

When cannibals are hungry, they say Chukwu is hungry.

When cannibals speak, they say Chukwu is speaking.

Now that cannibals want to eat me, they say Chukwu wants to eat me.

Chukwu will never allow them to eat me, so you must know that tradition is in the hands of cannibals.

Tradition is also history.

No one but the historian tells the history, and the historian of tradition is no one but the patriarch, Mbombog.

Historians only teach history. Patriarchs are historians who also narrate tradition.

But tradition is not only mere history but also energy, that is, the ability to put to action the capacity to create and destroy.

Therefore, tradition is energetic history, one that can create and destroy.

So, such a history must be coded before being transmitted to the public.

Tales are the coding of that energy, and myths are the encryption algorithm, the code of access to that energy – the supreme truth – to tradition.

Nri, sacrificing his two children to receive yam from Chukwu is just a story that never happened; it is a myth that veils the secret of tradition, life and the universe.

The Igbo people believe in the story of yam, and we, the people of Ngok Lituba, hold the story of the spider.

These stories are only tales, not facts. They are myths that openly convey the secrets of the universe and the ultimate truth to the wise while hiding it from the unwise.

Thus, the myth is the barrier that separates the known from the unknown, the finite from the infinite, the temporal from the eternity, ignorance from knowledge and life from death.

The myth itself is tradition. It is the universe, its big secret and the energy that created everything without being made.

To keep secret the energy that creates and destroys, ancestors created myths.

Through these myths, ancestors preserved and transmitted creative and destructive energy to the sages without putting it at the disposal of the bad ones. Thus, to the unwise, myth is a mere fact, but to the sage, it is a tale that veils the secret of tradition, life and the universe.

Tradition is not cannibalism.

Tradition is the knowledge of the universe transmitted from generation to generation.

Tradition is like a chimpanzee.

A hundred times, a chimpanzee falls. A hundred times, it springs back to its feet.

Like a fallen chimpanzee, tradition has fallen in Igboland.

Like a chimpanzee that returned to its feet, the great Igbo tradition will rise'.

As a sign of blessing, Biték joined his forehead with those of his sons. With tears welling in his eyes, Biték took the boat to Cameroon. Mr. Scott ordered his armed bodyguards to remain on standby until Biték disappears into the horizon.

This is how Biték returned to Cameroon in 1933.

Chapter 10
BITÉK RETURNS TO HIS VILLAGE

Biték escaped death in the Mbandi Attack, when he had an affair with the chief's second wife and in Igboland. It was evident that Biték was not running away from death. Instead, death ran away from him. Biték was unafraid to return to his village where he had an affair with the chief's second wife.

In 1933, Biték arrived at his village, and the whole village welcomed him. He went to the chief's house and asked for forgiveness. Kindap, the chief's second wife, was banned from the village, and nobody knew her whereabouts. The chief was already old and told Biték,

'My son, for so many years now, I have been waiting for this day to come so that I may forgive you and die in peace. Indeed, the words of our ancestors shall always come to pass. I was tormented by the idea of dying without making peace with you. So, I consulted Mbombog Ndjami to know if I would see you before I die. The Mbombog opened his Gambi and consulted ancestors on my behalf, and they revealed that you and I would meet again before I pass away.'

The chief took a kola nut and added,

'The kola nut symbolises the love between humans and divinities, as well as that among human beings.'

Then, the chief broke the kola nut into two pieces — one piece for him and the other for Biték — and said,

'Sharing this kola nut with you means that I have forgiven you. No matter how the teeth and tongue fight, they always forgive each other. Because they both know that the mouth is their only home.'

Then, Biték said,

'Human error has led to the belief that forgiveness is a weakness, not knowing that it is a prolonged force. We choose to forgive; therefore, we choose to be humiliated, scorned and deprived of our human dignity, and only strong men can make such choices.

Therefore, the weak in spirit will never be able to forgive. Forgiveness is the Olympic discipline par excellence of the spirit.'

While eating the kola nut and drinking palm wine, Biték shared his Nigerian journey with the chief.

Having eluded death several times, Biték decided to join the church to praise the Christian God. He joined the Presbyterian Church and became a church elder. Joining the Presbyterian Church was also a way for Biték to live a peaceful life and stay out of colonial trouble. The traditional religion Mbog was banned by colonial masters in favour of Christianity imposed by weapons. It was secretly practiced, and the Mbombog or traditional priests were killed. As such, many Mbombogs converted to Christianity to avoid being killed and preserve Mbog.

At the Presbyterian Church, Biték met a young woman named Bias, to whom he proposed. They eventually married and had 12 children. However, with their 11th child, Biték prayed to the Christian God and asked him not to give him any more children because he was getting old and had no more strength to provide for them. Biték also took his wife to Sakbayemi, an American Presbyterian hospital, where he asked an American doctor to stop his wife from conceiving, to which the doctor obliged. However, in 1953, Biték's wife got pregnant again and gave birth to a baby boy.

With the best palm wine and kola nut, Biték ran to the Mbombog to announce that his wife had given birth to a baby boy and know the child's name. The Mbombog opened his Gambi and consulted ancestors on his behalf. According to ancestors, Biték's baby shall be named Massocki, which means 'the last one', as his wife shall no longer conceive. The Mbombog repeated this to Biték, and his wife never conceived again.

CHAPTER 11
BITÉK SAVES THE NDOG MBOG VILLAGE

Biték ran away from the Ndog Mbog village in 1915 when Cameroon was under German occupation. However, upon returning to the village in 1933, Cameroon, his beloved country, was under French and British occupation.

When World War I broke out in 1914, aligning France and Great Britain against Germany, Cameroon, the German colony, was in a futile position, sandwiched between the British and French colonies.

By early 1916, the British and French took control of the country and divided it among themselves, and the Ndog Mbog village found itself under the French colonial empire. However, Biték only spoke his Basaa language and the broken English he learned in Nigeria.

In 1948, with the sole aim of gaining independence and achieving reunification for divided Cameroon by the colonial empires of France and Great Britain, 12 union members, most of them from the Ngok Lituba tribe of the Basaa people, gathered in Douala and created the Union of the Populations of Cameroon (UPC), a legal and political instrument conforming with juridical norms. Through the UPC and its secretary-general Ruben Um Nyobé, Cameroon's populace will make the will of independence and reunification they call Nkaa Kunde known to the United Nations (UN).

Through the UPC movement, the Ngok Lituba people became actively engaged in the independence struggle of Cameroon. Um Nyobé, father of Cameroonian independence and secretary-general of the UPC movement, also hailed from the tribe of Ngok Lituba, and his village was only about 60 kilometres away from the Ndog Mbog village.

The Ngok Lituba people proved total allegiance to the UPC movement. To ban the UPC after Um Nyobé's return from the UN, France incited a bloody uprising known as the Bloody Week of Douala (May 22–30, 1955) and blamed it on the UPC. Then, on the 13th of July 1955, the UPC was banned and declared a terrorist organization by France. Consequently, the UPC became a clandestine movement.

There were no more juridical and political means for the UPC to carry on with its independence struggle. As such, it had no other choice than to partake in an armed struggle known as San i Kunde by the Ngok Lituba people. The ancestral land had to be defended imperatively. Accordingly, the armed struggle for independence was pejoratively labelled as Maqui by the French colonial empire, and the freedom fighters were deemed maquisards.

In 1958, Um Nyobé was assassinated by France. Cameroon's nominal independence was proclaimed in 1960, and the drama revolved around the fact that those who did not want Cameroon to be independent and worked hand in hand with the colonial empires took control of so-called independent Cameroon. The French colonial empire installed as the president of the Republic of Cameroon its puppet, Amadou

Ahidjo, who ruled the nation from 1960 to 1982. In 1982, President Ahidjo was replaced by Paul Biya, another French puppet, who has been ruling Cameroon since 1982.

Despite the proclamation of Cameroon's nominal independence, the UPC remained illegal and clandestine until 1991. Its members were tortured and killed by the neocolonial government of President Ahidjo. The UPC movement understood then that the proclamation of Cameroon's independence was nothing but a facade, thereby refusing to recognise the legitimacy of French puppet Ahidjo as its president. Consequently, the UPC carried on with its struggle for the real independence of Cameroon, a struggle that was hostile to the neocolonial government and yet to be won until today.

Nationalist fighters of the UPC, labelled as the maquisards by France, proceeded with their armed struggle or Maqui against the French-installed government. In the Ndog Mbog village, there were three great maquisards: Wada Dominick, a son of the Ndog Mbog village; Seh Stanus Silas, son of the neighbouring village Ndog Hém; and Manyanog. These three maquisards sabotaged government installations within and around the Ndog Mbog village.

The maquisards lived in the forest, making their arrest and assassination direly challenging. Their fight was supported by villagers, although there were a few betrayers called 'Kokon'. The UPC became known as the immortal soul and regarded as part of Ngok Lituba tradition. Ba Mbombog, the traditional priests of Ngok Lituba, endorsed Maqui and conferred the maquisards with mystical powers.

With mystical power, the maquisards could disappear, become invisible, gain supernatural protection against gunshots and turn into trees and animals. This made it more difficult to capture and kill them. Thus, the myth of their immortality was born, inspiring more people to join them.

Many villagers who joined Maqui received mystical protection against gunshots and the secret of invisibility and disappearance. The mystical power of invisibility was called 'Dim Ba Ko'; the mystical protection against gunshots, 'Kon' and the mystical power of disappearance, 'Nlend Ba Sogol'. All these powers were conferred to the maquisards by traditional priests. However, these came with many rules to avoid transgression, or they would stop working. More importantly, these mystical forces had counterpowers.

To show that there is no such thing as mystical power against gunshots and deter people from joining the maquisards, President Ahidjo decided to kill Wada Dominick, Seh Stanus Silas and Manyanog. However, he knew that these mystical powers were real because he frequently visited traditional priests for protection.

To kill the three maquisards, President Ahidjo needed to know the counterpowers of their mystical protection. He took a Kokon (betrayer) who revealed them. For instance, to see an invisible maquisard, one must put secret liquid in his or her eyes.

One night in 1960, the armed forces arrived in the Ndog Mbog forest. They were guided by a Kokon who revealed where the maquisards were hiding. The Kokon dropped secret liquid in the soldiers' eyes, making the invisible maquisards visible. Then, the fight began between the armed forces and the maquisards.

That night, Manyanog was shot and killed. The fighting was so intense that the armed forces eventually retreated. Afterwards, the maquisards left the forest, went to the village centre and forced some villagers to go to the forest to dig a grave and bury Manyanog. Biték was among the villagers taken to the woods. It was so late that Biték made signs on the trees to mark and remember his way. Then, they dug a grave and buried Manyanog.

The next morning, the armed forces came back and brought the entire village to a vast empty field. Only the children were spared. The soldiers wanted the villagers to tell them where the corpse of Manyanog was buried. They were confident that they had killed him during the fight and wanted his body to prove that the maquisards were deceiving them and there was no such thing as mystical protection against gunshots.

However, fearing that the maquisards would kill them, the villagers claimed they did not know where Manyanog was buried. In response, the army commandant said to the villagers,

'As you are afraid to die in the hands of the maquisards, you will die in my hands.'

Upon hearing those words, the army then started beating and torturing the villagers, killing some in the process. The army commandant vowed to kill everybody if no one revealed Manyanog's grave.

In 1960, France created the Cameroonian Armed Forces with the sole aim of getting information about the maquisards through torture. The first director of the Cameroonian military school was a French lieutenant named Jacque Louis le Fedre, a renowned torturer. The Cameroonian Armed Forces specialised in this.

Biték was also taken; however, he was not tortured because he was a church elder. Church members were known not to support the maquisards. It was also well known that Christian Catholic priests were mercenaries and spies who actively worked with the colonial authorities. A Cameroonian bishop called Thomas Mongo played a significant role in the assassination of UPC Secretary-General and father of Cameroon independence Um Nyobé. In exchange for his role in the assassination, Thomas Mongo was designated as the first bishop of Sub-Saharan Africa.

Witnessing his people being tortured and killed, Biték decided to show Manyanog's grave. He sat on the ground, and next to him was a tortured villager with whom he had dug the grave. The tortured villager cried in pain. He bled out, and his face was disfigured because of the army's brutality. The man had no more energy left in him and was exhausted. Biték told him,

'I can't allow this to carry on. I am going to show them the grave of Manyanog.'

Before Biték could stand to call the army commandant to inform him of the whereabouts of Manyanog's grave, the tortured villager sitting next to him found the necessary strength to hold and keep Biték on the ground before he could move. The villager said to Biték,

'The grave of Manyanog is a symbol of human dignity and resistance against humiliation, oppression, repression, colonialism and neocolonialism. Torture must never force us to beg for mercy. We must die with our head high than live in humiliation and renounce Maqui. Let them kill us all, and, at least, our children will know what we lived and died for. Please let me die for the grave of Manyanog. Let me die for Maqui. There is no human dignity without courage. Let us stand the test and show courage to our children.'

To the tortured villager, Biték replied,

'Alive, we will teach our children about courage better than with dead bodies.'

He then stood and proclaimed loudly,

'If you stop beating and killing my people, I will show you the grave of Manyanog.'

The army commandant went towards Biték and answered,

'I agree to your terms, but if you waste my time, I will kill you.'

The army commandant asked his soldiers to go with Biték and ordered them to kill him should he fail to show the grave.

Biték was sent to the military truck and escorted with armed soldiers as they headed to the forest. The military truck passed by his house, and Biték saw both of his youngest sons, Massocki and Nonga, playing outside. He asked the soldiers to allow him to speak to his children before they continued, and they agreed. Biték told his children,

'It was very late at night, and I'm not sure if I correctly remember where we buried Manyanog. However, I left signs on the trees. If I do not find these signs, the soldiers in the truck will kill me in the forest. So, you may no longer see me again.'

Leaving his children in tears, Biték boarded the military truck again and headed to the forest with the soldiers.

Biték was already old. He walked slowly through the forest, and had difficulty finding signs he had left on the trees. The soldiers had been in the forest for hours. They pointed their guns at him as they started to lose patience. Biték said to the soldiers,

Many are those who know the whereabouts of Manyanog's grave but they have decided to die instead of showing it to you. Because the grave of Manyanog is a symbol of human dignity and resistance against humiliation, oppression, repression, colonialism and neocolonialism.

I am your only hope to find the grave of Manyanog. You kill me and you will never find it and you will never be able to deter villagers from joining the maquisards.

I am not afraid to die because showing you the grave of Manyanog, I already chose to die in the hands of the maquisards. Put down your weapons and allow me to find the grave.

Biték took six hours to find the grave. Then, the soldiers said to him,

'You are fortunate, and you just saved your village.'

The body of Manyanog was exhumed and taken to the army commandant. He later presented and exhibited Manyanog's dead body to the entire village, telling them,

'Biték is your hero. He saved all of you. There is no mystical protection against gunshots. Here is the dead body of Manyanog, who received five bullets to his chest. Stop allowing yourselves to be deceived by the maquisards. Cameroon is now an independent country. We are no longer under the French and British occupation. The French and the British are no longer our enemies. They are our partners. The enemies of the state are now the maquisards. We will hunt them wherever they may be and kill them."

The whole village was freed, and they chanted Biték's name. However, Biték knew that the maquisards would kill him after his betrayal. Thus, he went home, gathered his whole family and told them,

'To have courage is to take action with knowledge of the deadly consequences they may have, and to be responsible is to face them head-on. These are what I would like to teach you. I am 78 years old now. I have no more strength to run away. I can neither swim the *rivers of crocodiles nor climb hills. Moreover, I do not intend to leave my family again and die in exile. I want to give you the chance to see my dead body. Prepare for my funeral as the maquisards are coming. You know where to bury me. I will never regret the choice I made. It was imperative. I did not intend to betray the maquisards, as Maqui is a noble and legitimate struggle. If I happen to die in the hands of the maquisards, I do not want you to remember me as someone they have killed but as someone who courageously died for Maqui. I want you to remember me as a maquisard as well.'*

Three days later, the maquisards visited Biték. Seeing the maquisards enter Biték's house, the whole village gathered in prayer outside. They cried, and they were against the maquisards killing him. Suspense filled the area; the villagers did not know what was happening inside the house. Was Biték dead or alive? No one knew for sure.

One of the maquisards peeked through the window and saw the villagers outside. He said to his fellow maquisards,

'The villagers are outside, and they don't want Biték to die. If we kill him, we will lose their support.'

Inside the house, the maquisards addressed Biték.

'We have come to kill you. Say your last prayers.'

Biték responded,

'I did not betray the maquisards. The maquisards betrayed us. They told us a lie. They told us that there was mystical protection against gunshots when there was none. Did you expect me not to show Manyanog's grave and allow genocide to take place only to preserve the myth and legend of mystical protection and immortality? Are myths and legends worth a genocide? They are extremely destructive when misunderstood and taken literally. Myths and legends have turned the Igbo people into cannibals. Because of the mythical tale of yams, the Igbo people eat one another. For the sake of a legend of immortality by the maquisards, you want to sacrifice a whole village. This legend you want to preserve is more dangerous than colonialism; it has killed more of our children than colonialism has. You can kill me now, but leave my children alone."

To prove to Biték that the mystical protection against gunshots was real, Wada Dominick, one of the maquisards, removed his gun, gave it to Biték and asked him to shoot any of the maquisards.

Biték told Wada Dominick,

'I do not believe in mystical protection against gunshots, so I will not shoot. Moreover, when I ran away from this village because I slept with one of our chief's wives, I made a promise to Nsas Nanga that if he let me cross the river, I would never be a hunter again, and I would never kill again.'

Then, Wada Dominick retrieved his gun from Biték and shot his fellow maquisard, Seh Stanus Silas, thrice. However, no bullet touched the man, and the bullets bounced like tennis balls against the wall.

Upon hearing gunshots, the villagers outside Biték's house all screamed, *'Biték is dead!'* They started crying and fell to the ground.

After having shot Seh Stanus Silas, Wada Dominick told Biték,

'Mystical power against gunshots is neither a myth nor a lie. We do not deceive our people. The government and the French colonialists deceived you. They invaded our land, destroyed our tradition, customs and rites, killed our ancestors, stole our wealth and installed their puppet, Ahmadou Ahidjo, as president of the Republic to carry on with colonisation. You betrayed us, but at the same time,

you saved our village. We will no longer kill you. However, we will take everything that belongs to you in this house, including your animals, goats, sheep, cats and dogs.'

Chapter 12
BITÉK SHEDS TEARS

1966 was the most painful year in Biték's life — a year he remembered until his last breath. In that year, Biték lost his first son who was twinned and born to his second wife.

In the city of Edea, some 10 kilometres away from the Ndog Mbog village, Bias Bi Biték was violently killed by a speeding truck on the side of the road, killing him on the spot.

The news of his son's death stabbed Biték's heart like a dagger. It was one of the few occasions where Biték remembered having shed tears in his life.

Upon hearing the news of his son's death, Biték went to the Presbyterian Church where he was an elder, got on his knees in sorrow, opened his Bible and read the Book of Job.

'I came out naked from my mother's womb, and naked I will return to the womb of the earth. The LORD has given, and the LORD has taken away; blessed be the name of the LORD.'

Still on his knees and in tears, Biték prayed.

'We give birth to children so that they will take care of us in our old age and bury us, not the other way around.

I am burying my son, the same one who was supposed to bury me.

Oh, God. My life has turned upside down.

May Bias be the last son I bury. If not, take me now so that I do not bury my sons anymore.

God listened to Biték's prayer, and Biték never buried any of his children again.

CHAPTER 13
BITÉK'S LAST WORDS

Towards the end of the '60s, Biték began to lose his eyesight. As he was impoverished, he could not afford medical care. In the early '70s, Biték had become completely blind. He could only recognise people through their voices and permanently needed assistance.

Biték was so poor that he could not afford shoes. He always walked barefoot and shirtless and wore a loincloth that he tied around him. He had one or two shirts that he only wore on Sundays to church.

He lived in a wooden house almost entirely broken down by termites. The roof had holes, and the place was flooded nearly every time it rained.

Biték had boundless love for Massocki, his youngest. He always said that he would not die without Massocki finding work and building him a house. Biték also swore that he could not die if his last son was not beside him.

In 1975, Massocki visited his blind father in the Ndog Mbog village to tell him that he had been recruited to the civil service as a customs officer. Biték was thrilled to hear the news. However, he cried when Massocki told him that he had been transferred to Cameroon's northern region, where then–Cameroon President Amadou Ahidjo was originally from.

The nationalist and independent movement UPC, based south of the country, refused to recognise the legitimacy of Ahidjo's government as it was neocolonial. In 1955, the colonial power France declared the UPC a terrorist organization and banned it until 1991.

During the wars for independence, those who killed UPC fighters based south of the country were northerners generally known as Houssa, with mercenaries from Chad, Cameroon's northern neighbour.

The UPC's secretary-general and father of Cameroon independence, Ruben Um Nyobé, hailed from the Ngok Lituba tribe in the country's southern region. Naturally, nationals from the south, especially when they were from the Ngok Lituba tribe, were considered UPC members and, therefore, terrorists. That is why Biték cried upon hearing that his son had been transferred to the north that was in favour of Ahidjo's government.

Biték told his son Massocki the fable of the gorilla and the woman.

Once upon a time, in a village called Ndog Djéé, a mother had to work the land with her newborn son every morning. Upon arriving in the field, the mother had no one to look after her newborn son. The gorilla took pity on her and said, 'Let me take care of the baby while you work the land, and the mother kindly accepted the gorilla's offer.

Every time the mother worked the land, the gorilla would quietly take care of her baby. The gorilla told the woman that he would always look after her child if she kept it a secret, and the woman promised.

However, one day, the woman's husband became curious and asked his wife how she could work and take care of her baby at the same time. Contrary to the promise she had made to the gorilla, the woman told her husband that a gorilla took care of her baby while she worked the land. The woman's husband then informed the entire village of this. As such, the villagers decided to kill and feast on the gorilla.

One morning, the mother carried her baby and went to work the land. However, she was unaware that her husband had been following her with a shotgun, accompanied by the entire village who wanted to kill the gorilla.

When the mother arrived at the field where she worked the land, she found the smiling gorilla waiting for her. The gorilla greeted her, and as usual, she handed over her child. While the gorilla was playing with the baby in its arms, the husband pulled out his gun to shoot the gorilla but mistakenly shot the baby and killed his son. The gorilla turned to the woman and said, 'What comes out of your mouth is what kills your child.' Leaving the mother in tears, the gorilla dropped the dead child and fled into the forest.

After he finished telling the gorilla fable, Biték told his son,

'As the gorilla says, it is what comes out of your mouth that kills your child. If the woman had kept her mouth shut as the gorilla had asked, her child would

not have died. I represent the gorilla, while you represent the woman who works the land. Meanwhile, your life represents the woman's child. During your stay in the north, as long as you keep your mouth shut, refrain from talking about politics and the UPC and refuse to give your opinion on these issues, you will come back alive. No one needs to know your opinion and what you think about life. If you keep your opinions to yourself and not try to change the world, you will live long and in peace.'

Then, Biték added,

'When tradition is passed on to the new patriarch, he is given Jai Li Mbog, which symbolises the visible world and the power to rule that world. The transmitter of tradition holds Jai Li Mbog in his hands. With all his strength, the receiver of tradition is asked to take Jai Li Mbog from the transmitter's hands forcefully. Have you ever wondered why the transmitter of tradition has to hold Jai Li Mbog firmly in his hands and why the receiver of tradition has to take it forcefully from him?

The transmission of Jai Li Mbog symbolises earthly life – a life characterised by injustice and the perpetual struggle for justice. We live in an unjust world, so even with taking what rightfully belongs to us, we must use force and, sometimes, at the cost of blood. That is why the new patriarch must forcefully take what belongs to him.

When the lion kills its prey, on which side does justice and injustice fall? If we lived in a just world, nature would have made all animals vegetarians. You must know that justice is a belief and a religion, and we cannot force everyone to adhere to such. Once you understand all of this, you will keep your opinions to yourself. By doing so, you will live long and in peace. You, who will take up your position in the north of the country, listen to the gorilla, and shut your mouth because what comes out of your mouth is what kills you.'

When Biték finished, he locked foreheads with his son as a sign of blessing and told him, *'Fear not. You will come back alive.'*

Six months later, Massocki returned home from the north with his first salary to start renovating his father's house, which took over two years to complete.

In 1978, Massocki visited his father to celebrate the end of the construction. He brought food, drinks and a new loincloth as his father had asked him to. Massocki entered the house and greeted his blind father, who recognised his voice. They ate and drank, and when they were done, they sat down to talk. Biték said to his son,

'Now that the house has been built and you are here, my time has come. When I die, you and your mother must not cry. As soon as I die, you must go and call my cousin Togo Bi Son. You and Togo will have to wash my corpse and clothe me. When all of this is done, then, you will announce my death to the village.'

Massocki told his father that he understood and would carry out his word. Then, he asked his father, *'How do you know that your time has come to an end?'*

'Because our ancestors are in front of me. They came to get me. The first time they visited me, I begged them to wait until you had found work and built me a house, and they agreed. They guaranteed I would die in your arms', replied Biték.

Then, Massocki asked his father,

'You're blind. How could you see our ancestors?'

To this, Biték replied,

'Those who only have eyes to see are the truly blind. Ancestors are the eyes of the living. They reveal themselves to whoever they want and show what they

want whenever and in whatever way. Indeed, the soul belongs to ancestors and the body to the world. He who runs in every man perishes his life, just as the soul that runs in all souls perishes its spirit. I return to Ngok Lituba, and I do not fear death, as the staff of ancestors guides and protects me.'

These were Biték's last words. Soon after, the elderly man fell into the arms of his son and died. Massocki carried his father's body and lay it in the bedroom. Then, following his father's will, he ran to call Togo, his father's cousin. Togo and he washed Biték's corpse, dressed it and then announced his father's death to the village.

Chapter 14
TESTIMONIES

O n the 1st of September 1978, at the age of 96, Biték died from old age, and his youngest son, Massocki, covered his corpse. He left 1 or 2 widows, 14 children, and several grandchildren.

According to tradition, anyone who dies beyond 90 is considered to have lived long enough on Earth. Therefore, at his funeral, people did not gather to mourn and cry; instead, they celebrated and wished him farewell.

At his funeral, similar to his birth, a traditional sect of women known as the Koo came to dance the Koo dance and narrate his life. The Koo women recounted the good and the bad in Biték's life.

For the good side of his life, the Koo women testified that Biték was a quiet and lovable person who will always be remembered by the people of Ndog Mbog for having prevented genocide in their village.

For the bad side, the Koo women vouched for Biték's life filled with romantic aspirations. The following is a testimony of a Koo woman.

'Biték loved women, and women loved him. He slept with most women in this village. This testimony holds my admission that I slept with Biték. He was irresistible. Any woman could immediately fall in love with him just by looking into his eyes. He was a man who women fought for. It seemed like Biték had a secret key that opened the hearts of all women and secret words that got all women to fall in love with him. I still remember the first words Biték had said to me as if it was yesterday, and those got me in his bed.

I was bathing in the Pume Stream, and Biték was passing by. Standing on the bridge, he set his eyes on me while I was naked. Looking at his eyes shining like stars, I could not find the courage to tell him to stop looking at me, as if I was hypnotised by his charm. It was at that time he uttered words I will never forget.

"You are the measure of beauty.

No one has defined beauty before having met you.

Not even the Mbombogs, our wise men, can define beauty until they meet you.

Your beauty is beyond that of marine spirits.

They say the waterfalls of Song Lolo are the attraction of our village.

I disagree. You are its attraction.

Whoever sees you would no longer want to see the waterfalls of Song Lolo.

You are a remarkable view.

You are a garden.

Your breasts are the sweetest of all fruits.

Any man who looks at you gets goosebumps.

The caresses of your hands can heal any sickness.

You are perfection.

Only Hilolombi creates perfection.

You are the living witness of Hilolombi, the most ancient of ancients.

Right now, if you ask me to jump, I will."

These words consumed me, and without hesitation, I asked him to jump. Biték jumped into the Pume Stream, and we made love on the stream's rock. When we finished, I said to him,

"We made a transgression; it is against our tradition and custom to make love on the rock."

Then, Biték replied,

"Customs and tradition do not apply to you. The transgressions of this village's people are as many as the grains of sand in the sea. You are the only one stopping the fury of ancestors from destroying this village."

I replied,

"That's blasphemy. Stop speaking of ancestors in vain."

Biték said,

"Our gods made you the most beautiful and desirable of all women. To see you and not desire you is what is considered blasphemy against our gods."

All of you gathered here today at the funeral of Biték, do not judge me prematurely and say that I was an easy woman. I was not. Was our chief's second wife also an easy woman when she fell in love with Biték? Was Bias also an easy woman when she did? What about Bell, Tom, Job and the others? Were they easy women as well? We were not. Biték only had a special, unique charm.

We are not here today to judge Biték. As it is said in our tradition, we do not judge dead people. Instead, we have gathered here to bid him farewell and pray for him to be received in the land of our ancestors and reunite with Ta-Ra.'

CHAPTER 15
THE EXISTENTIAL QUESTION

Biték pushes us out of our comfort zones by questioning our preconceived answers to existential questions on concepts such as destiny, life after death and so on.

Does destiny exist? This is an existential question each of us has asked ourselves at least once in our lifetimes and for which we all have different answers.

Biték's life seems to answer the question of destiny with certainty, as the concept of his life and death was fixed upon his birth and his life's journey predicted by his ancestors.

Although Biték's life seems to have affirmed the existence of destiny, his life cannot be an absolute answer to this question. As one of our ancestral sayings goes, 'The gorilla does not run away from what someone else has seen.'

In the end, Biték's life remains an enigma, a mystery and a labyrinth of questions.

References

Echeruo, M. J. C. (1979). *A Matter of Identity.* Ahiajoku Lecture, Owerri: Culture Division, Ministry of Information and Culture.

Manus, U. C. (2007). The sacred festival of Iri Ji Ohuru in Igboland, Nigeria. *Nordic Journal of African Studies, 16*(2), pp. 244–260.

Metuh, E. E. (1981). *God and man in African religion: A case study of the Igbo of Nigeria.* Geoffrey Chapman.

Ogbalu, F. C. (1979). *Omenala Igbo: The book of Igbo custom.* Varsity Industrial Press.

''*He who runs in every man perishes his life, just as the soul that runs in all souls perishes its spirit.*'' — Biték

CPSIA information can be obtained
at www.ICGtesting.com
Printed in the USA
LVHW092310240821
696052LV00002B/62

9 789956 465095